Beyond Speciesism

Poems by
Flavia Ursino Coleman
& Friends

Copyright Flavia Ursino Coleman and contributors 2020©

All rights reserved. Apart from fair dealing for the purpose of private study, research, criticism or review permitted under Copyright Act 1968.
No reproduction, copy or transmission of this publication may be made without written permission.

First Published in Australia by USNCOL Pty Ltd,
188 Scenic Highway, Terrigal, NSW 2260 Australia.
monkeybusinessthebook.com
colemanpublishing@outlook.com

eBook ISBN: 9780994271648
Paperback ISBN: 9780994271655
Kindle ISBN: 9780994271662

Book Cover Design: Rasel Khondokar
Book Formatting: Rasel Khondokar

A catalogue record for this work is available from the National Library of Australia.

Dedication

To all beings of feather, fur, fin and skin,

that they may live free of suffering

&

To my wonderful grandchildren,

Jacob, Oliver and Isabella

that they will live in a world

beyond speciesism

Acknowledgments

To my wonderful husband Kevin for his hours of help and humour.

To my daughters Laura and Crystal for their support.

To all inspiring animal rights activists, who have given and continue to give of themselves tirelessly through the long, dark night as the truth is exposed.

To those who have and continue to open my eyes.

To those who have contributed their amazing poetry:

Les Thompson, Matt Stellino, Trish Haywood, Susan Sentient, Ralph Graham, Rochelle Wood and Peg Parish.

To Clare Mann for her guidance and for writing the foreword for this book.

To Celine Esnault for editing and layout.

To Bee Morgan for my portrait.

To Kathy Divine for her help and advice.

A huge heartfelt thank you to all.

Foreword

Clare Mann

Vegan Psychologist and Author of Vystopia:
The Anguish of Being Vegan in a Non Vegan World.

As I write these words from my office in the Blue Mountains, I observe a thick, choking smoke outside my window; evidence of the devastation wreaked by weeks of the worst bushfires Australia has ever seen. At the time of writing over twenty people have been killed and the world rightfully mourns their death and the loss to more people of their homes, communities, and belief in a bright future.

Almost a billion native animals have been reported dead, either burnt alive or from starvation and thirst after habitats were destroyed. Yet farm animals do not get such a respectful farewell. The media reports "stock losses," and the army called in to build mass graves. Anecdotal reports are heard of farmers locking paddock gates, so farm animals can't leave and losses can be substantiated for insurance purposes.

Why are there such differences in how we perceive the value of different species? It's called Speciesism: the assumption of human superiority that leads to the exploitation of animals. It encompasses differing treatment of animals; those we regard as friends and those we regard as food.

All beliefs, including speciesism, are based on socially and culturally determined myths. Beliefs can give hope and the vision of a better future. They can also keep people stuck in repeated patterns that cause great unhappiness, ill-health and loneliness. Beliefs change over time as new information becomes available and myths are dispelled.

For example, people once believed the world was flat and that the four- minute mile was merely a pipe dream. The medical world rebelled against the concept of germs creating illness, until it eventually became an accepted medical fact. And all of this is based on beliefs.

Flavia and others, who will meet in these poems, live in the hope of our speciesist beliefs changing. They dream of a better future for all sentient beings, a world in which human superiority has no place and animals have lives for their own sakes. These poems echo our collective desire to live in harmony with all animals and Mother Nature. They are exquisitely written, although in places painful to read, but awaken the archetypal memory of non-speciesism residing within each of us.

Join me in becoming reawakened to a world we have forgotten and which, by changing our beliefs, we will see again. Together, as Flavia says, we can all have that quiet prayer answered: that the sun one day will rise on a planet that values the sacredness of all life in all forms, however they may show up.

Clare Mann

Like so many people I once claimed to love animals, to care about my health, to pride myself in being a spiritual person, to care about the environment and my children's future.

Like so many people I was hoodwinked by the veil of industry secrecy.

Then one day the truth became shown to me. I learned that animals, health, spirituality, the environment and my children's future required me to live a life of integrity in alignment with my values. I was playing in the shallows and I needed to become vegan.

You see, it's all about being non speciest and the ethics of non-selective compassion.

Going vegan was, and is, the only path that aligns us with our higher selves.

Contents

Love Them Don't Hurt Them 1
In Their Memory.. 2
Unforgotten 3
Born To Be Wild 6
Little Spider 7
Pretty Bird 8
No Lives Lost 9
One With Life 10
Circus... 11
Life On The Inside 12
Tourism 14
Pest 15
Kangaroo 16
Brumby 18
Orangutan 20
How We Treat The Voiceless Speaks
The Loudest To Who We Are 21
Racehorse 22
The Crowd 24
Greyhound 27
Gentle Giant.. 28
A Tale Of Two Cats.. 30
Happy Backyard Hen... 32

Rooster	33
Fly Sweet Angel, At Last You're Free	34
Duck Out Of Water	36
A Spiritual Gift	38
Rationality	39
Live Export	40
My Sweet Mama	42
The Day The Truck Came	44
Love Is Love	46
Death Row	48
Saying Goodbye	50
Gates Of Hell	52
Against Their Will	54
Can't Stomach Cruelty? Go Vegan!	57
Rip, Tear, Steal	58
Fish Cannot Scream	60
Vegetarian	61
Lobster	62
Prawns	63
Animals Don't Give a Damn What We Eat as Long as it's Not Them	64
Words	65
To The Land	66
Xenotransplantation	68
Animals Carry Our Karma We Must Be Nice To Them	70
They Knew Not Why	71

Count The Cost 74

Economy No Eco No Me 76

We Must Come To Our Hearts Or Perish 77

Lessons Learned Since Being Vegan 78

The Master's Flute 80

Activists Are Optimists 82

Once Upon A Time 84

Love Your Children? Save Their Planet Go Vegan! 86

Spirituality Equals Non-Selective Compassion 87

For The Curious 88

Other Publication 89

Love Them Don't Hurt Them

Flavia Ursino Coleman

In Their Memory
by Flavia Ursino Coleman

It's in their memory that I write

I lie awake and pray at night

It's in their memory with sword held high

That their rights to freedom I'll not deny

It's in their memory that my soul doth yearn

Humanity awakens and seeks to learn

It's in their memory of those lives taken

That our remembrance of them, not be forsaken

Unforgotten

A smile rose on my face, effortlessly, unguarded, spontaneously. I had not realized, although the stranger to whom I'd bemoaned the state of the world said. "Your face just lit up with the brightest smile at the mention of animals?" Her statement and question in one.

As she sat awaiting a reply, I wondered how to convey the joy they bring, and the love I feel for all angels in feather, fur and fin. "I just love them" - I wanted to say.

Several images flashed across my mind; a bittersweet compilation.

I thought of all the times I've leapt out of bed and sprinted up the stairs at two am to spy the possums that scurry across our balcony.

I thought of how I've stood motionless by the side of the road watching cows in pastures protectively gather around their young. Their desires no different to my own maternal desires. Their fate, in the hands of man.

I thought of how no morning is ever so rushed, that I do not delight in being stopped by ducks that cross in front of my car.

I thought of dolphins held in captivity, trained to understand and to respond to up to fifty human words, and how no human has yet managed to learn one single word in dolphinese.

I thought of a hen, and how she clucks to her young before they are born to her warmth.

I thought of the skillful dexterity of a pregnant sow, and how she prepares for her young with a bed that enables escape from her crushing weight.

I thought of the baby bat high in the tree, throwing tantrums when mama has to leave in order to forage for food, and the babies whose mamas will never return.

I thought of sheep, and how they can identify up to a hundred of their friends from a photo of just part of a horn.

I thought of the magical colour of fish, and the pleasure they get from rubbing against certain objects.

And then my thoughts dimmed. I remembered once witnessing a brave mother mouse defending her pups as she stood on her hind legs beneath a grown man's shovel.

I remembered why I protest so hard in the streets, banners raised high, hoping that someone, anyone, will hear the voice of the Voiceless.

I remembered the letters I'd written and posted to authorities, asking they be gentle with our humble brethren.

I remembered the Mardi Gras floats, marching through the streets dressed as a cow, a chicken, a bunny. Dancing for the freedoms that they may never know.

I remembered the rescue hens, and their promise of a forever happy home where they can bathe in the sun, and scratch in the dirt. Their dignity and their lives spared.

I remembered the talks that I had given at spiritual forums, telling all that the time had now come for non-selective compassion.

I've wondered late at night, as I've laid awake with a quiet prayer, if the sun will one day rise on a planet that values the sacredness of all life, in all forms, however they may show up.

I've wondered what it will take for a man to find the courage to ask if he values that piece of meat, or a woman her leather handbag, as much as that animal might have valued his or her own life.

It has been said, that which brings great joy too may bring great sorrow, but in that moment I just wanted to speak of my great love.

Yet, I did not know where that love came from, why I love or how I love, I just knew that I loved somehow. So I sat quietly with a continued smile.

Two or so days had passed. I stood watching our two year old grandson. A familiar smile lit his face, effortlessly, unguarded, spontaneously. He had just spotted an animal.

In that moment, I had come to realize the only difference between myself and that stranger that day, was that I had never forgotten.

Flavia Ursino Coleman

Born To Be Wild

Wild animals born to be free

Building their nests high up in trees

Flying over and dwelling in seas

They do not belong in captivity

Flavia Ursino Coleman

Little Spider

Little spider

Clothes line rider

Dear little spider with a web so fine

Attached so neatly to my clothesline

How many hours did it take to spin

Fastened at edges and woven within

A tight curled leaf that serves as your home

Tucked at the centre of your hunting zone?

We can't share the line for there's not enough space

But I don't want to move you in any case

For such a construction deserves to stay

So I'll dry my washing some other way

In memory of Peg Parish

Pretty Bird

Oh pretty bird, how sweet you sound
Perched inside your metal surround
The wild as your home, you'll never claim
But it matters not, having learned your name
You need not forage for days on end
And know not predators from which to defend
Your wings clipped so you'll stay by my side
Warm and dry you'll live inside
Oh pretty bird I must scurry away
We'll talk some more some other day

Flavia Ursino Coleman

No Lives Lost

Bushfires swept across the land
Heroic firefighters with job in hand
Trees ravaged exploding high
Determined they'd see not one soul die

Wildlife fled
Or so it was said
Neighbours rallied with hoses high
Fighting fires of blackened sky

Thousands of acres all too soon lost
Charred remains their only cost
Sweltering heat met with a sigh
Humans and houses saved, not a soul did die

With much remorse I see beyond
And ask of my fellow creatures, of which I am fond
Their lives not counted in the final cost - why?
I shed tears amongst their ashes, as I say goodbye

Flavia Ursino Coleman

One With Life

I am one with life

Interdependent on all of life

Therefore, I will defend all life

With my life

For the rest of my life

Flavia Ursino Coleman

Circus

Roll up, roll up, roll up!
For your fleeting pleasure
Donkeys and horses and lion pup
No better way to enjoy your leisure

Tonight's fun line up will entertain
Chimp in outfit up high wire
Elephant released from her chain
Tigress jumping hoops of fire

Treated well like family you know
Held in cages and travelled far
Eager to see you at the show
To welcome centre stage our latest star!

Flavia Ursino Coleman

Life On The Inside

Roll up roll up. The circus is in town!
There's a huge coloured big top and smiley faced clowns,
By starlight it's coming! The bright poster said-
With exotic wild animals (of course all captive bred),

Fun to be had for all, and more -
There's a world of wonder and magic and awe …
Come through the doors and see all the sights!
We even have lions that don't ever bite!

The lights are bright - the stage is set,
For an evening wonder - all hopes must be met …
But away from the crowds sits a monkey in a cage –
He doesn't look happy. I don't know his age …
But his eyes tell a story, of sadness and pain
And the small space he's stuck in - just drives him insane
He remembers a life when he had a family -
they now long gone - this now his reality.

He climbs the bars and goes to the right -
He does the same thing over till late each night –
Some trees to make a nest is where he should sleep –
But instead it's a steel cage - it makes my heart weep

There's nowhere to run and nowhere to hide -
It's so different for him, when it's seen from inside.
One rope is the one thing he's been given to use -
But he still searches the cage for a possible way through ….

He looks up weary, so tired of it all -
He's been here since he was so very small.
They make me do things that I don't like –
Wear nappies and ride ponies and bikes.
He just wants to be treated like a monkey as he should.
But humans had to get everything out of him that they could.

Now he's older and therefore can't breed -
In reality he now costs them more just to feed
His days are numbered and this hellhole's Big Top –
Perhaps maybe one day we will be able to stop –
Using animals for our own use and fun -
Only then will our fight be won.
Please don't buy a ticket to these shows,
If you plant a small seed -
From that something big grows -
So please spread the word about kindness to all,
Because this planet belongs to all creatures great and small.

Rochelle Wood

Tourism

Elephants are not rides
It hurts their backs
It's what tourism hides
So we don't attack

Tigers in temples
They are drugged for your leisure
They are not items to assemble
They are dear souls to treasure

Monkeys shouldn't dance to amuse
Treated like prisoners of war
Chained, beaten, and abused
They belong with their families who they adore

Animals do not belong
Behind wires and chains
It's all sad and so wrong
Time to look behind the veil of tourism claims

Flavia Ursino Coleman

Pest

While you were sleeping
We were weeping

You destroyed our home
To build your own

Our lives shattered
Our family scattered

Confused we roam
Scared and alone

Without a nest
We're declared a pest

We come to your door
For ours is no more

Don't pull out a gun
Just think what you've done

Flavia Ursino Coleman

Kangaroo

I've looked into her bewildered eyes
A displaced confusion she cannot disguise
From her carer's bag being carried around
A far cry from mum, who once bounced on the ground
Sucking her toes, she wears away their tender pads
Comforting herself for missing the mum, that she once had

I've seen the burnout on her carer's face
Her love reflected through each tender embrace
As she feeds her orphan around the clock
Gently stroking away her horrific shock
There'll soon come a time to let her go
Will she survive? We'll never know

I've heard that carers thin on the ground
With not enough hands to go around
Countless hours, are they in vain?
How can man, be this insane?
Slaughter of our majestic emblem; what a disgrace
Disbelieving eyes of the world, watching this space

I've heard the cracks in our first man's voice
"They were here first", he states, "it should be their choice."
He tells the tales of the mighty Roo, here long before man
'It's their birthright to claim this great southern land'
The carnage, the bloodshed, and his broken heart
Listening to our Aboriginal elder's plea, tears me apart

I've read the trembling hands surrounded each night
They cannot sleep, and wake in fright
A war zone, a living hell, guns blazing away,
Roos fleeing, their babies dying, as gentle souls pray
No land safe of such thinly disguised greed
Blood streaming into rivers from which gunmen feed

I've seen the blood lust of man protecting his stock
Claiming to love and care for his grazing flock
Bravely ridding himself of all competition
So man can devour their flesh, after all it's all just tradition
Yet all animal's lives matter, of this I've no doubt
Please open your eyes, see with your heart, and give a loud shout

Listen to mother earth and her broken beat
Her shattered heart, cracking beneath our feet
For when in time her tears will fall
In her deluge we will but call and call
For we are her offspring, and she our fate
Stand with me now, before it's too late

Flavia Ursino Coleman

Brumby

From a distance I could hear screams, terror and crying
It was a chilling confusion that night, that led me her way
I looked down on earth upon the agony of those left dying
Around me souls in different coats, yet as one we began to pray

A magnificent creature stood silently watching me
Gingerly, I bowed in approach with an outstretched hand
An eerie mixture of relief and confusion I could clearly see
Though without words, we each the other, so deeply did understand

She'd awoken from a nightmare, or perhaps worst still
Gentle in her being, she'd been a victim of violence
Of the cold indifference of man asserting his will
I dropped to my knees before her, and her foal, in remorseful silence

As a majestic brumby in foal claiming her home in the wild
She'd run freely, approaching her time of giving birth
Her beating heart was that of a mother carrying her unborn child
The same maternal love, shared by mothers across the earth

That day, choppers reigned terror from the sky
Her friends screaming in horror, as for their lives they each fled
Tears in my eyes and shame in my heart, I could not tell her why
Man had boasted victory, as in agony they each slowly bled

Her defenseless unborn had died kicking inside
Unable to protect nor comfort, she fought for life to the bitter end
The only place he could, but for a short while hide
I had no words for my fellow man's actions, nor could I even begin to defend

I changed her name from pest to innocence
Neither she, nor I, could such massacre comprehend
Man's blood lust and eagerness to kill simply made no sense
My mind stopped searching for answers, as I continued to comfort my beloved friend

I awoke with her in my heart as she laid on my mind
She and her foal, with whom I stayed up all night
Longing to change the hearts of men, with the words I struggle to find
Vowing to continue in her name, having known her bravery, and her gentle might

Flavia Ursino Coleman

Orangutan

Their eyes met
Hers pleading from inside the net

Their home chopped down
Clutching each other to the ground

Her maternal love so deeply protective
Killing her was his first directive

The orangutan hunter paid so handsome
The broken mother grasping for her son

Fighting against their fate
Pumping her chest hoping he'd relate

In her dying moments she pumped her last drop
Milk her son needed, begging the horror to stop

Yet wealthy folks had other plans
To have her baby in their hands

Making way for cheap palm oil
Such greedy use of forest soil

Flavia Ursino Coleman

How We Treat The Voiceless Speaks The Loudest To Who We Are

Flavia Ursino Coleman

Racehorse

Did you watch as I ran that race
In your glamorous hat with champagne in hand
Dressed to the nines in delicate lace
Dancing with excitement as you screamed from the stand?

It seems I won that race for you
My owners boasting and counting the cash
Taking off your heels for that party they threw
Recounting over and over my final dash

You jumped for joy yelling my name
Laughing and anticipating my number call
Repeatedly whipped again and again
Broken, I stumbled in my fatal fall

That very night all the papers read
How it could have been so very much worse
"Thank God", they wrote, "nobody's dead"
No longer alive to make millions, their only curse

Yes, you watched as I ran for my life
Yet not for one moment did you see
Blood in my windpipe, painful joints, ulcers and strife
Or that I was drugged, stabled, lonely, and seldom free

You heard my number, but you did not listen at all
Or you would have heard my pitiful distress
In agony veiled behind that green screen wall
I died, while you danced in your party dress

The excitement you felt, was yours not mine
Watched but never seen, as they made a killing
Heard but never listened to, you believed all was fine
You missed that I was a sentient being, and never willing

Flavia Ursino Coleman

The Crowd

The people were excited in the stand
Today, the rodeo has come to town
They shouted as they watched a country band
Soon they'll see the cowboys hit the ground

We stood behind the gates, talking
to our stable mates
Dreading that electric cattle prod
Glory is all theirs and for
us the pain and fears
Waiting for the man to give the nod

Their egos going mad
Don't they know it's sick and sad?
I hope that I survive out there today

My little brother's young and not so fast
I hope he don't get hurt and makes it back
They chased him and outpaced him
The rope went 'round his neck
That was when we heard that deadly crack

The whispered words were spoken
My brother's neck was broken
Laying still in the dust and sweat
We cried and we jeered
But the people yelled and cheered
It's about as bad as it can get

You put that money down you think you own us
Body, mind and soul just your big toy
While families shouted loud
He lay beneath a dusty cloud
My brother died that day just for the crowd

The cowboys raised their beers and ate their steaks
"How long did you stay on?" was all the go
The injured and the dead are soon forgotten, party time
"It's a shame I guess, when's our next show?"

They love us very much, they're so sad to put us down
Just sign the papers, buy another round
"Look, I know it's sad of course
but he was just a bloody horse,
Now he's saved the pain of getting old"
"I'll take you into town we'll put the money down
A brand new horse, you'll be good as gold"

You put that money down you think you own us
Body, mind and soul just your big toy
While families shouted loud
He lay beneath a dusty cloud
My brother died that day just for the crowd

My brother died out there, just for the crowd

Someday, you will see, it's more than sadness
One day your heart will turn around and say
"I won't buy the tickets thanks, I see the madness"
A horse or calf will live another day

Ralph Graham February 2019

Greyhound

At last I run free with my own pack
Trying to make sense of my life upon which I look back
Perhaps you can answer some questions and tell me why
As I search for answers from high above the rainbow sky

Why did I have to earn my keep just to stay alive?
Why did my slower siblings not earn the right to survive?
Why did I always hear, "oh but greyhounds just love to run"
And assume my old barren cage was a whole lot of fun?

Why did man not see my begging to be by his side
As his lifelong companion filled with such pride?
Why did he taunt me to rip apart possums and piggies
And not see how much I wanted to play with those kitties?

Why did he force me to give all those births?
Why did he choose those worthy to live on the earth?
Why did my injured babies fill each shallow grave
And not see in my heart my desperation to save?

And when I was too sore and slow to run for my life
Did he send me to the brutality of the researcher's knife?
I've so many questions I know, and even many more
For the species I was born to love, trust, and adore

Flavia Ursino Coleman

Gentle Giant

Disorientated, he ran towards the burning light
Running from his captors, to the jeering crowd's delight
While center stage the matador stood so brave and proud
Whipping up a frenzy, from the blood thirsty crowd

The frightened gentle giant had been held inside a box
Tormented by his captors from behind hidden locks
Vaseline used liberally to blur vision from his eyes
Newspaper in his ears, and cotton up his nostrils to snuffle out his cries

A strong corrosive solution on his legs gave greater pain and more
Too painful to stand, even more to walk, unable to lay on the floor
A needle inserted into his genitals as any gent will tell
Is the greatest testimony to all, there exists a living hell

Amongst the mass hysteria he did suddenly recognise
The one who'd bred and raised him as his winning prize
The gentle giant approached seeking to be relieved
The bond they'd shared together, in which he still believed

Each towards the other, they both made their way
The gentle giant assured himself, he'd finally get away
That crowd, pleasing moment far too tempting to resist
His breeder rewarding his audience, with that show stopping kiss

It was the kiss of Judas, that final kiss of death
Taunted, the gentle giant knew, that there was nothing left
A torturous end awaited, as he fought for his life
Repeatedly blood squirting from a sharpened knife

The gentle giant that night, lingered till he died
His groans of agony drowned out by the crowd's orgasmic high
Yet the knife that pierced his heart, was not the deepest of them all
As his eyes searched the crowd, it was not he, who fell from grace, in his final fall

Flavia Ursino Coleman

A Tale Of Two Cats

My regal friend of mystery
She tells her tale through history
Of love and friendship, fear and foe
Her place in my heart she'll always know

By end of Stone Age, she was by our side
Hunting mice with regal pride
For saving the food that we had stored
My little moggy became adored

Now we all know of Egyptian times
When to hurt or kill her was a crime
Worshiped as a Goddess throughout her life
Laid to rest with stores of mice, for her afterlife

In China and Asia she was believed magical
After all, who'd dare argue she not mystical?
Romans and Greeks had her domesticated
Her valuable companionship authenticated

By Middle Ages all was dim
Declared an agent of the devil, her life then grim
By papal orders almost eradicated
Burning her alive, the church vindicated

For she was nocturnal, and roamed at night
Evidence of supernatural powers the devil's delight
Her family throughout Europe had all but perished
I guess my dear friend, was no longer cherished

Ah, but then the Black Plague struck its evil curse
Wiping out countless from the universe
My beloved friend was not around
To clean the rodents from the ground

By late 1800's she was put on show
Again her beauty we'd come to know
Long haired cats considered best of all
Competing for prizes in major stalls

And as the centuries have rolled on by
I sit in awe watching her as I sip chai
While many folks claim her a pest
I argue otherwise in loud protest

For she is the tale of two cats
A loving presence who worships my lap
Or the greatest pest who roams with dark pride
Just ponder upon history, before you decide

Flavia Ursino Coleman

Happy Backyard Hen

Oh happy backyard hen

Another egg you've known to lay

Living inside a well-built pen

We generously give you our scraps each day

As part of our family we give you care

And not allow predators to harm you by night

A blessed exchange for the eggs you share

So we can bake cakes and foods to delight

Though sometime soon there'll come a day

When your egg laying days are cast behind

We'll open the gates and allow you to stray

Setting you free to your own kind

Flavia Ursino Coleman

Rooster

He crows his song to the rising sun
Strutting his iridescent plumage to its rays
Amongst subtly melting dew on a new day begun
His majestic existence amongst its haze

At his sight I bow in reverence
His regal demeanour, stirs me deeply within
As quietly I am stilled by his presence
Humbled by privilege of bearing witness to him

Many a folk shun him as a noisy inconvenience
After all he does not earn his keep to suit their needs
In angry tone they show no lenience
A fictitious hierarchy which man's ego feeds

They realize not, or perhaps care less still
That roosters such as he are considered industrial waste
Bouncy day old chicks in hatcheries tossed in a mill
Macerated alive, for they produce no eggs nor flesh to taste

Flavia Ursino Coleman

Fly Sweet Angel, At Last You're Free

Shattered spirits and broken bones
Left to die by the side of the road
The truck driver making good speed
For time equals money, and money equals greed

Cars screaming by and the terror you felt
Born a battery hen, a bad hand dealt
I cannot say if I cry for you, or cry for me
Maybe I just cry for all those years I could not see

Hatched in a tray without a mother's love
Never her natural warmth or that of the sun
Never allowed to scratch in the dirt all around
Or make yourself a dust bath on the ground

De-beaked by noisy machines right at the start
The agony you felt tore you apart
Your entire life forced to stand in a wire cage
I never understood, but now I rage

The pain you lived as you struggled to eat
Covered in infections from head to feet
Your burning skin coated in waste
No one noticed, they just grew you in haste

They didn't care about your broken legs
Your only value to them were your eggs
They stole from you until you were spent
Space needed for the next, so off you went

Tossed like rubbish you were sent to die
Scared and thirsty you didn't know why
Crammed with your sisters on the back of a truck
When at roaring speed the road you struck

Spared the horror of a loud production line
Upside down you'd see the world one final time
A loveless place heartless and cold
To which you were born, to which you'd be sold

Should in your final moments have struggled for life
Jerking your head and missing that knife
A worst fate would have been your moment of slaughter
You'd have been boiled alive, in a tank of scalding water

Your body dismembered or perhaps not
For a dollar or two, they could sell the lot
Void of dignity, your corpse displayed
Better never born, for with your life you'd have paid

Still here in my arms you take your last breath
Your only relief is to finally meet death
So fly sweet angel, at last you're free
Your gentle soul, the world could not see

Flavia Ursino Coleman

Duck Out Of Water

I need water. I'm going blind
My eyes oozing beneath crusty infection
While scratching causes them to constantly sting

I need water where I can be with my own kind
To glide with pride through my graceful reflection
A place to play, and splash, and stretch my wings

Yet I am confined, cramped, and overbred to grow
Dragging beneath the burden of my weight
My life in their hands over which they have power

Tired, I close my eyes to a place I long to know
I dream beyond the pain in a tightly packed crate
Knowing not what awaits as I languish each hour

I need water so that I can float
My legs too fragile to constantly stand
Aching like they are breaking beneath my body

I need water so that I can glide between boats
A place to frolic and paddle and dry off on land
I am sentient, not something but somebody

I long for a place where I can be who I ought to
Somewhere beautiful and safe where I can swim by shore
Where I can wash away my blisters, burning skin and broken heart

To no longer be a duck out of water
I'll know nature as I've never known her before
I'll make a nest and babies and a brand-new start

I overheard that at first light I'll be taken from here
Away from this filth I'll bathe in a sunlit stream of water
And I'll proudly cross the road with ducklings in toe

But now first light has broken and I only feel fear
Trucked for hours across scorching state border
What comes next I do not know

Finally arrived at my destination scared, lonely and thirsty
Roughly shackled, I'm hung upside down for slaughter
Blinded by crusted eyes, legs tearing off my oversized flesh

Workers blinded to their souls, mock and laugh at me without mercy
Terrified I pass not through a sunlit stream, but a stream of electric water
My wretched life you may in time meet, wrapped in plastic, labelled fresh

Flavia Ursino Coleman

A Spiritual Gift

I asked a mate for two sheep so I could stop mowing the grass
Dick arrived with five sheep on the back of a ute
We opened the back ready for two to jump out
The other three headed for the butchers
I gave the two names, Tango and Cash
It didn't take long a loving bond had begun
They came when I called, each running
At five months to the day at six thirty-five am Cash came calling at the back door
I went out. "What's wrong Cash?" She slowly turned around
I saw a baby's nose poking out
As I followed, she'd stop to turn towards me to make sure that I was there, as she led me to the right place
Out came a lovely boy lamb I named Frankie
Two days later at five forty am at the back door there was Tango calling
"What's wrong darling?"
She turned to reveal two feet poking out, so I again followed, and Johnny was born
Now the four have made my life so much richer

I am blessed!
And yes, they made my mower redundant

Les Thompson

True story

Rationality

A wonderful word
until it is used to rationalise
that which is not rational

Flavia Ursino Coleman

Live Export

The scorching earth seared her last day
She resisted being dragged with what little she had left
Had she been stronger, perhaps the rope might have given way
Forty days of monstrous waves meant she had not slept

On foreign land she'd been beaten off a live export boat
In vain she searched for some sign to reassure
Somehow, she had managed to survive afloat
The sickest of her friends thrown overboard, she'd see no more

Those too timid could not reach water nor food
Trampled they drowned in a sludge of faeces and urine
The stench suffocated the ship with an angry mood
To the workers no sheep had individuality to define

As if someone had turned up the oven on fifty degree heat
Her lungs burning in the boot of a stranger's car
The pulsation of her wounds intensified as ropes cut into her feet
Surely this was not how it was meant to end, given she'd come this far

Weather extremes throughout her life were often unforgiving
During biting winters, the wool off her body humans would steal
Seen as nothing more than a commodity not someone living
Unwilling to see in her eyes, just how she did feel

Memories kept flooding of neglect back home
Forced to give birth in the freezing cold
Each frost-bitten death she mourned all alone
What became of her stolen babies she was not told

They were products of artificial insemination
Long rods poked into her vagina inserting semen
Never given pain relief during or after implantation
Each of her handlers behaved as if they were a demon

She knew too well the terror her young ones felt
As they huddled together bleeding and shivering
Blades cut muscle, bone, tail, all the pain they were dealt
Helplessly watching as each stood quivering

In her last moments she could smell the blood and the fear
She thought of her friends and wondered what had become
The slaughterman held his saw, and she knew death was near
She thought of her babies, and prayed for each one

Flavia Ursino Coleman

My Sweet Mama

My sweet mama, I'll not cross over yet
Not while your tired feet are aching
And your tender heart's breaking
Our few stolen moments, we'll never forget

My sweet mama, they're calling my name
I'm no longer a number or referred to as veal
Or the product of rape and a tragic ordeal
Yet sweet mama, you loved me the same

My sweet mama, soon I'll cross to the other side
A far nicer journey than the one I just had
Born a boy got the farmer real mad
Slamming me onto a truck for a long thirsty ride

My sweet mama, soon carefree I'll run
It won't be sad, like watching you run after me
Weary from birth it wasn't to be
Humans stealing your milk, and leaving me none

My sweet mama, my friends all together now play
As babies we trembled before the slaughterman's knife
Quivering my heart stopped as blood drained from my life
Your heart beating loudly, led me back to you all the way

My sweet mama, I'll soon cross our time cut brief
While you will again be forced to give birth
Milk, ice cream and cheese, to them your only worth
With silver they'll pay, while you with your grief

My sweet mama, the rainbow bridge it shines so bright
I'll cross with a piece of your heart to light my way home
And when your time comes mama, I'll not leave you alone
As together we'll walk, through that bright shinny light

Flavia Ursino Coleman

The Day The Truck Came

"What's it like being loved?" asked the cow over the fence.
Taken back, doggie didn't hurry to reply.
"Like being told that you are good without begging or pretense?"
Doggie tilted his head. "Maybe farmer will love you if only you try."

Big, brown cow hung her head low
"I get yelled at, kicked and chased as a milking machine."
Doggie gave a whimper. "I'm sorry, I just didn't know.
Just following farmer's command, your sadness unseen."

"But you hear me bellowing for my babies for nights on end
You've never wondered as you've sat cozily by the fire?"
Doggie fell at cow's feet. "Nipping at you, I cannot defend.
Farmer ignores your grief, so I never understood the love you desire."

"My sadness feels like it will never leave
My babies stolen with only mastitis to take their place.
They induced my last birth after I was raped to conceive
The vet injected me with a needle then vanished without trace."

"Why that makes no sense," doggie protested.
"Farmer didn't want to waste time on me rejoining the milking herd
To him I am just a commodity in which he's invested."
The two became inseparable till the day the truck came
and cow left without further word.

Flavia Ursino Coleman

Love Is Love

I saw a butterfly today
She landed on my nose
We stared together eye to eye
And great respect was grown

My life was bleak, a horror show
But today I learned to love.
She's a bug and I'm a pig
But love is love you know.

She came to me again today.
I wonder if she knows?
The day is near that I must go.
The day I'll face my foes.

But that was then, and now is now.
And now I love her so,
her colours of bright gold and black,
Warms my heart to glow.

The human came and kicked me hard,
My stomach hurts me so.
But there she was just fluttering near
And I was soothed to know

Today's the day they'll take me to the place
We all must go
The place so bright with blood and fear,
Where no-one wants to know.

I long to see my love once more,
To strengthen my resolve.
But no such luck for me today,
My luck has run low.

A man in white will hit my head,
And cut me ear to ear,
Out will flood my precious blood,
My heart will beat with fear.

I had my thoughts, my feelings too,
But that means naught to him,
And not one bit to the person
who on my flesh will gnaw and binge.

As my life ebbs away,
I think of my sweet love,
And hope we'll meet beyond this place
Where wrong and evil's done.

Trish Haywood

Death Row

She was born on death row
On a cold concrete floor
The only home she'll ever know
As countless to come, as countless before

She's a victim of violence
Who's committed no crime
Condemned by our silence
She serves out her time

For consumer demands her rapes repeated
Her body so broken she can barely stand
Birth after birth she remains defeated
Knowing never a kind word nor gentle hand

Helplessly she watches her piglet's mutilation
Writhing in agony beneath a sharp blade
Teeth clipped, tails cut, and genital castration
Then tossed like rubbish not gently laid

Unable to suckle the weakest die
Slow painful deaths and worst for those found
Picked up by guards who make their way by
Who legally smash their heads on the ground

The strongest join the cycle of abuse
Prisoners behind consumer bar code
Sold to the public as items of use
As tasty products amongst shopping load

Addicted to flesh and taste
Lied to by industry to make such choices
Told it's OK as long as there's no waste
Nothing wasted but precious lives with unheard voices

Once we see beyond the walls of our hearts
We the prison guards behind each endless excuse
Awaken to our humanity a brand new start
Closing behind forever, those gates of abuse

Flavia Ursino Coleman

Saying Goodbye

We met briefly, then I had to say goodbye
You weren't going on a holiday, you were going to die
When I saw you I could tell, you knew something was wrong
This place was unfamiliar and you didn't belong

I hope you found solace huddled with your kin
Unaware of the impending act of sin
I hope you died quickly and were free from harm
But having seen how this place murders, my hopes are in vain

I know your final moments were filled with terror and fear
Even though I couldn't be with you, your cries I did hear
Although the physical act committed was by the slaughterman's knife
Those really responsible are those who put their taste buds over your life

Now your body hangs shackled and lifeless
They will try to claim your murder was akin to bliss
Some people will take you home from the supermarket shelves
Saying they respect you, but only thinking of themselves

I'm so sorry this happened to you, I know it wasn't fair
You were betrayed by the very farmers who always claim they care
The truth that nobody wants to know
It's all just a big act, a front, a show

They never cared for you only the money
This is the truth I ask people wake up and see
So one last time I say goodbye my friend
I will fight for you, until the fight ends

Matt Stellino

Gates Of Hell

We approached the gates of hell
Towards a pristine sunrise
Mesmerized we stood in its spell
Trepidation betrayed by our eyes

All too soon first light had broken
Eerie silence giving way to blood curdling screams
Holding our breath not a word was spoken
Facades crumbling into tears of streams

Brave men attempted a joke or two
Holding flowers women dropped to the ground
Kneeling in helplessness it was the best we could do
Amidst souls squealing those gut-wrenching sounds

As captives they'd known a life of terror and pain
Macho devils relishing in cowardly power
Over innocent beings without as much as a name
Thrashing in gas chambers in their darkest hour

Cooking from within they remained undead
Their hearts still required to beat
Hooked by a leg, throats slit so's to be bled
In order to be packaged as healthy, white meat

That day we walked away with our backs to the sunset
Unable to speak our hearts trailing behind us
Each night we kneel for those we cannot forget
Your bacon, ham and pork there to constantly remind us

Flavia Ursino Coleman

Against Their Will

They smell the blood
They feel the fear
The loss of life
Their end is near

Held in cages
Held in mud
Those courageous
Tears of flood

Terrified now
The bird and pig
The goat and cow
Trapped in a rig

With kicks and prods
A terrible thirst
Their killer nods
And grabs the first

With violent slashes
The screams begin
With stabs and gases
Merciless sin

A slippery tread
Skin, blood and guts
Stored in a shed
'Consumer cuts'

STOP the carnage
STOP this dread
STOP this killing
STOP we said

Supply, demand
Is your command
What you drink and what you eat
Turns feelings into meat

You have a choice
They have no voice
The life you buy
The compassionate cry

What have we become?
Why do we succumb
To profit driven
Scandalous scum?

Chose right now
To take a vow
To stand up strong
Against what's wrong

Susan Sentient

Can't Stomach Cruelty? Go Vegan!

Flavia Ursino Coleman

Rip, Tear, Steal

Rip, tear, steal
Skin taken against their will
Dogs and cows skinned alive
For frivolous fashion to thrive
Such a lovely fashion trim
Casually bought on a whim

Knife, stab, club
They want their fur without the blood
To enter the room in such a manner
That turns each head to their glamour
The smell of dollars hard to resist
While consumers allow, they'll persist

Rip, tear, steal
Without a thought of how they feel
Feather down so cosy at night
Ripped from their skin they cannot fight
Ostrich plumage colours so magic
To the birds themselves so very tragic

Knife, stab, club
From the cow's aborted bub
For its much sorted treasure
The softest of all slink leather
The pain beyond imagination
For which there is no justification

Rip, tear, steal
The torture deadly real
Wool, angora, cashmere
Animals living in fear
It's time to think twice
For they pay the price

Ready, set, go
As cosy and nice
Let's all chose faux

Flavia Ursino Coleman

Fish Cannot Scream

How would you like to pass some time
With idle chatter as we cast a line
Soaking in sunshine while we wait
Knowing, that sooner or later, they'll take the bait?
Tempting morsels on a hook to be taken
Our catch of the day will have mistaken
We'll reel them in just to brag their size
The neighbour's dogs, our winning prize.
Casting our line over the fence
Claiming it's sport our best defense.
We'll let them loose once we reel them in
For us and the dogs it's a fun filled win.
They get exercise as they run from us
It's our recreation so what's the fuss?
Or then again, on second thoughts, far better still
Let's hook a fish, it's a painless kill.
Unlike the neighbour's dogs, fish cannot scream
Those who argue otherwise, are far too extreme!

Flavia Ursino Coleman

Vegetarian

You're a vegetarian you so proudly state

Though, you do reserve room for fish on your plate

But fish are not vegetables, they do have a face

Perhaps you'll consider something different,

to take fishy's place

Flavia Ursino Coleman

Lobster

Please do not mistreat me or boil me alive

I'm a lobster, a crustacean, I cannot go into shock

I'll feel prolonged scalding while I survive

Excruciating pain that I simple can't block

Flavia Ursino Coleman

Prawns

Time to celebrate

With prawns on a plate

To meet demand they mutilate

Industrial dollars do dictate

Cutting out their eyes to mass procreate

Demand industries no longer hide, what's on your plate

Flavia Ursino Coleman

Animals Don't Give a Damn What We Eat as Long as it's Not Them

Flavia Ursino Coleman

Words

Words used to justify

Who should live and who should die

Who should thrive

And who to deprive

Flavia Ursino Coleman

To The Land

George could not bring home the bacon
Cause he was sick as a dog
He did give a rat's don't be mistak'n
His memory like a goldfish he laid in a fog

In a country that rode on the back of sheep
His father's father ran heads of cattle
When dark days fell and the world was bleak
He rode his war horse into battle

His beast of burden by his side
In a trench too small to swing a cat
Still like a lion he held his pride
Though he was go'n blind as a bat

Returning home when the war was over
He and his girl loved like rabbits
Having gone cold turkey from his lover
Though hungry mouths made em change habits

Commotion escalated to many a cat fight
She dreamed of many more fish in the sea
While he laid counting sheep at night
Stubborn as a mule she cut herself free

Now George's father on the other hand
Chose he'd not be such a goose
Going through life with a back-up plan
When women got his goat he'd cut em loose

With such poor role models George went through life
Joking and laughing and being a ham
Instead of warring with his wife
He took his rifle to the land

Flavia Ursino Coleman

Xenotransplantation

Why do you have me reduced
To nothing more than your organ warehouse
As spare parts for humans that you have seduced
With Frankenstein experiments conducted in-house?

Such elaborate term xenotransplantation
I am a hybrid. I am in part pig and in part man
As a man-made creation I offer this simple explanation
You mistreat your organs, and I carry the can

These organs, they do not belong to me
Nor are they yours that I'm made to grow for your use
They're a DNA combination of both of us of us you see
Your life is of value, mine of abuse

You've weakened my immunity to tolerate their growth
Sentient man or pig I am not either
I am a complex formation of both
Yet for my suffering and despair you care neither

You have given me greater intelligence and deeper insight
And what I see in not the depth of your humanity
I see your darkness as I weep through the night
You've shown me not your dignity, but your depravity

Harvesting the organs of my sisters and brothers
You behave without conscience and great disregard
Profitable outcomes, pretending that of choices, you have no others
Yet the greatest price will be yours which you do not regard

For what you have sown you will in time reap
Yourself you will destroy as you weaken my offspring
I am an innocent being and revenge I do not seek
You are blinded to what your endeavors will bring

Your technology allows nothing to counteract what is endemic
I carry retroviruses of a different species indeed
Through me you have opened the door to your future pandemic
For the demise of your offspring, you have now planted a seed

Flavia Ursino Coleman

Animals Carry Our Karma We Must Be Nice To Them

Flavia Ursino Coleman

They Knew Not Why

They lived in quarters cramped
In windowless houses void of fresh air
No sunlight to kill the rotting damp
Broken and penniless souls in despair

With no internal plumbing nor refrigeration
Rubbish and sewerage filling streets below
Where tales were shared of dark desperation
Of sores and infections, they'd come to know

As with the living, the dead bathed in stench
Bodies in streets, steams and houses in putrefaction
Rapidly amassing to fill each trench
Awaiting weeks for doctor's certification

From slaughterhouses, to houses doctors did scurry
Examination of meat, the living and the dead
Then off to those in labor they'd hurry
Unwashed hands, delivering babies from their mother's beds

Motherless babies who survived their births
Condemned as wretched child slaves
Working crushing machines beneath dusty earth
Amongst the countless were too few saved

Suspicion amongst neighbours did quickly spread
As deadly disease gave chase, they knew not why
We compare to those dark early days with dread
Reflecting little as to why they did die

Fast forward to our great modern times
With pride in our eyes we make frantic claim
That we have no time to cherish, enjoy and unwind
For to declare other would bring great shame

Yes, indeed we now have refrigeration
Spilling easy meals, food-like substances minus nutrition
Of animals and chemicals and industrial creation
Endorsed, not examined nor viewed with suspicion

In our modern world many a child is born
With tens of thousands of chemicals long banned
Floating toxic soups swimming through their umbilical cords
As industries hide while mothers are slammed

In today's modern world where farmed animals dwell
In windowless houses fresh air and sunlight void
Undercover footage exposing their hell
Living in infestations they cannot avoid

Disease spread through birds, fleas and mice
In shared squalor animals condemned to die
Meds and jabs, chasing each to their graves for a price
While industry shrugs claiming, they know not why

Expanding houses, slaughterhouses and deforestation
On a planet we will soon be unable to save
We look upon neighbours with suspicion of causing infestation
Scientists with meds and jabs, chasing each to our graves

Flavia Ursino Coleman

Count The Cost

Take ten minutes for reflection

In order to make a true connection

For what you are about to read

Are those taken to feed man's greed

In a short ten minutes it's hard to believe

Those whose souls we do not perceive

Their individuality permanently lost

Look beyond the numbers and count the cost

Flavia Ursino Coleman

Wild fish caught	Over 18 million
Chickens	Almost 2 million
Farmed fish	800,000
Ducks	58,000
Pigs	29,000
Rabbits	22,000
Geese	13,000
Turkeys	12,000
Sheep	10,000
Goat	8,000
Cattle	5,000
Rodents	1,300
Pigeons and birds	1,100
Buffalo	500
Horses	90
Donkeys	60
Camelids	60

Economy
No Eco No Me

Flavia Ursino Coleman

We Must Come To Our Hearts Or Perish

Flavia Ursino Coleman

Lessons Learned Since Being Vegan

1. The term 'strict vegan'. If I don't buy from the meat, dairy, egg and honey sections of the supermarkets I may just starve. Thank God for my front lawn.
2. Raising vegan kids is extremely dangerous. Hospital wards would overflow with malnourished vegan children. Thankfully there is McDonald's in the foyer of the Children's Hospital.
3. Jails are full of angry vegans.
4. Doctor's surgeries have line ups of vegans requiring protein injections.
5. The billions of dollars in the health industry is entirely supported by vegans lacking vitamins and minerals.
6. In spite of the billions spent advertising animal products, it's vegans who ram their cruelty free message down everyone's throat.
7. It's a personal choice to take away the choice of animals who want to live free of cruelty and harm.
8. Plants feel pain equally to animals. It's devastating to see neighbours mow their lawn!
9. Humans are the only mammals that will lose their bones if they don't breastfeed from womb to tomb. Those who love us lose their minds when we stop suckling.

10. Animals who give up their lives for humane slaughter are the shyest. There is not one single image of them marching to their humane slaughter over the net. Not one!
11. If we don't eat them, they'll eat us. Imagine being chased down the road by a hungry lamb.
12. Sooner or later I'll be stranded alone on the same island with millions of other vegans.
13. Meat eaters are at the top of the food chain. Strange I though bacteria was. Umm
14. All a happy ending, when we thank those dismembered animals on our plates for willingly giving up their lives, for nothing more than a ten minute taste sensation. Just as God intended!

Flavia Ursino Coleman

The Master's Flute

I bare my soul to you
As before you I stand
A moment of intimacy known by so few
Different life forms on a foreign land

I've come to know you as too myself
Sacred forms through one life streaming
Denial of the other is the denial of self
For we are of the same origin beaming

Having arrived here in different forms
Disguised only by feather, fur, skin and wing
Tunes of the one flute upon which the master performs
To each assigned our own sweet notes to sing

I know your pain as I do my own
Your desire to live with freedom of presence
To nurture your young and to build your home
To live in peace and to express your essence

For each we breathe of the very same air
Born each to the same mother earth
As she lays herself open for each to bear
Different but equal to each she gives birth

Yet nowhere is it written that man should control
For dominion is of the ego's deception and lies
A shattered reflection and no longer whole
The master's flute falls silent as each note dies

Flavia Ursino Coleman

Activists Are Optimists

Activists are optimists

No time to be a pessimist

Holding placards high

The message you'll read in their eye

They inspire with voices loud

Marching alone or in a crowd

They'll endure ridicule and blistered feet

Turning each corner and walking each street

Their message simple and clear

Which they will tell you without any fear

For they know that silence is consent

To an unjust system to which they'll not bend

For the only thing necessary for the triumph of evil

Is that good men do nothing and allow great upheaval

They cannot bear to see such harm

By those high ranking with wrongful charm

They live with bellies on fire

Acutely aware of their greatest desire

A world to rise in conscious evolution

Fairness and compassion a new world solution

Portrayed through their movements and voices

A new way to live through conscious choices

As they all know that now is the hour

For the power of the people, is greater than the people in power

Flavia Ursino Coleman

Once Upon A Time

To my beautiful grandchildren for whom I now write
Longing nothing more than to commence, by penning
'once upon a time'
But time is running out, so we must now all do what's right
So that perhaps in time you may commence, by writing that classic line

I hear your laughter bitter-sweet in a world dying fast
Your carefree dance devoured by lies on which we've all been fed
That humans are the greatest and that somehow, we'd all last
Without care for sentient beings, on plates on which they're bled

Trees yours to climb, may soon be bulldozed to the ground
Countless species lost and many more we'll never meet
So adults can graze on flesh, as they drink another round
Lying to innocent hearts, deserving far more than deceit

And as I observe your flushed cheeks playing in a world ravaged by fire
Your sweaty foreheads running as all around rivers dry
I fight against evil from my soul's maternal desire
For it's from you we've borrowed this planet, til the day we die

Perhaps in time we'll speak of what was once another time
I'll wipe away my tears for your soul's greatest wisdom yet
I'll know of your compassion for each and every kind
As singers sing and poets write of past with deep regret

You may think of animal cruelty and those purpose bred
And hear shameful whispers of rivers almost dried
For billions of sentient beings til finally bled
Water stolen for them as industries schemed and lied

You may in time look back on earlier generations
And ask questions and exclaim, "But how? That makes no sense!"
And you may hear of heroes across many nations
Who gave their lives fighting for victims in their defense

Or you may simply pen those words which I deeply so desire
You may indeed commence, by writing 'once upon a time'
You may write for your offspring your soul's urge stoked by fire
Reminding those to follow, as you choose that classic line

Flavia Ursino Coleman

Love Your Children? Save Their Planet Go Vegan!

Flavia Ursino Coleman

Spirituality Equals Non-Selective Compassion

Flavia Ursino Coleman

For The Curious

MONKEY BUSINESS: A STORY OF SOULMATES AND PRIMATES
monkeybusinessthebook.com
BOOK BY FLAVIA URSINO & KEVIN COLEMAN

Other Resources

SavePoppy.com
Cowspiracy facts
What The Health facts
NutritionFacts.org

Other Publication

Monkey Business: A Story of Soulmates and Primates

Written as a romantic/suspense, Monkey Business: A Story of Soulmates and Primates examines the ethics of biomedical research and animal experimentation. Explored through the eyes of cub journalist Estelle Goldstein, daughter of pharmaceutical executive Sam Goldstein, and granddaughter of psychic, animal rights activist Esther Harris, this witty 'faction' provides a story beyond the mainstream narrative.

Chosen for presentation at The Byron Bay's Writer's festival 2016, Monkey Business: A Story Of Soulmates and Primates makes for compelling reading that dares to challenge the conventional worldview.

www.ingramcontent.com/pod-product-compliance
Lightning Source LLC
Chambersburg PA
CBHW030454010526
44118CB00011B/936